SACAGAWEA

By Betty Westrom Skold

5269

DILLON PRESS, INC.
MINNEAPOLIS, MINNESOTA

©1977 by Dillon Press, Inc. All rights reserved

Second printing 1978

Dillon Press, Inc., 500 South Third Street
Minneapolis, Minnesota 55415

Printed in the United States of America

Library of Congress Cataloging in Publication Data

Skold, Betty Westrom.
    Sacagawea.

(The Story of an American Indian)
    SUMMARY: A biography of the Shoshoni woman who
acted as interpreter, intermediary, and guide to the Lewis
and Clark expedition across Louisiana Purchase lands in
1804 and 1805.
    1. Sacagawea, 1786-1884—Juvenile literature. 2. Shoshoni
Indians—Biography—Juvenile literature. 3. Lewis and Clark
Expedition—Juvenile literature. [1. Sacagawea, 1786-1884.
2. Shoshoni Indians—Biography. 3. Indians of North
America—Biography. 4. Lewis and Clark Expedition]
F592.7S1237   970'.004'97   [92]   76-30613
ISBN 0-87518-095-7

ON THE COVER:

*Although this Shoshoni woman and her baby were photo-
graphed in 1878, they look much as Sacagawea and Pompy
did when they traveled with Lewis and Clark more than
seventy years earlier.*

SACAGAWEA

The Lewis and Clark expedition (1804-1805) was
organized by President Thomas Jefferson to explore the
newly acquired Louisiana Purchase lands and establish
an overland route to the Pacific Ocean. As an interpreter
and guide for Lewis and Clark, the Shoshoni woman
Sacagawea provided invaluable assistance to the expedition
and served as a symbol of the peaceful intentions
of the explorers.

Contents

CHAPTER I

Sacagawea's Beginnings

Sacagawea stood alone on a gentle rise overlooking the brown river. Black hair hung in two thick braids over the beaded yoke of her buckskin tunic. Her lean body was approaching womanhood. Sadness clouded her brown eyes.

There, far below, lay the Missouri River like a great stout rope coiled around the grassy hills and off beyond the sunset. It was a rope which could lead Sacagawea from this place of captivity back to the land of her beginnings. At the age of twelve she had been captured in an enemy raid and carried away from the land of her people, the Shoshonis.

It was natural that the Missouri River should remind her of her childhood home in the Rocky Mountains, known to the Shoshonis as the Land of the Shining Mountains. The river was born in those mountains and churned and wriggled its way eastward through this place on the prairie. From here it flowed southward all the way to Saint Louis.

The land of Sacagawea's childhood was a beautiful country. Shafts of sunlight shone down through evergreen trees, which hugged the sides of snow-crowned mountains. Cold rivers thundered over rocky beds, and great sheets of water

Land of Sacagawea's childhood.

broke in glittering foam over the falls. Mountain meadows
were bright with flowers.

Sacagawea, the daughter of a Shoshoni chief, was born
in 1788 in what is now known as the Lemhi Valley of
Idaho. According to tribal history, the name given to her
was Bo-i-naiv, the Shoshoni words for Grass Maiden. Sacagawea was not her Shoshoni name, but was given to her by
the Hidatsa people after she was taken prisoner. Sacagawea,
meaning Bird Woman, is the name we know her by today.

While Sacagawea was still a baby in a cradleboard, the
promise was made to another Shoshoni family that one day
she would become the wife of their son. Her father had
received several horses to seal the agreement, according to
tribal custom. For the Shoshonis, marriage was far too

important for their survival to be left to chance.

As a child she loved to hear stories from the old ones of her family. A leaping campfire would burn down to crumbling coals as Sacagawea, her sister, and her two brothers asked their grandparents questions about the history of their people. They loved to hear about that time long past when their people were first known as Shoshonis, "the people who live in the valley."

The Shoshonis were descendants of lake dwellers, who many years before had moved up from Mexico and settled in a great fertile basin between the Rocky Mountains and the Sierra Nevadas. The earth gave richly, and life was easy, but as many years passed the rains no longer came to water the land. Lakes dried up, game animals either starved to death or moved up into the mountains, and the Basin became a barren, treeless desert.

The Shoshoni people were forced to change with the changing of the land. No one place offered enough food for all of them, so they began to live in small, scattered family groups. They became nomads, no longer living in one place, but moving from place to place in search of seeds and roots, fish, birds, and small animals.

The Basin Dwellers learned many lessons from the harshness of their land. They learned to know which plants and animals could be safely eaten, which roots had a pleasing taste, at what time of the year the berries were ready to be picked. Journeys were planned so that they could eat each plant as it ripened. Life was lived in harmony with the changing seasons.

The land taught them to wear clothing that was right for each season. In summer the men and children wore no clothing at all or a breechcloth of badger hide, while the women wore an apronlike garment of hides. Sandals were woven from the fibers of the yucca plant. Warmer clothes were needed for the bitterly cold desert winters. Jackrabbit skins thrown over their shoulders like a cape were belted at the waist. They wrapped their legs in leggings made of hides and wore badger hide moccasins.

Makeshift shelters of brush called wickiups suited the life of these desert nomads. Why should they use their strength to build a fine shelter when they would be moving on in a few days? Home was wherever the berries were ripening, the roots were ready, or the grasshoppers and jackrabbits could be found.

After the rain clouds had gone, no large game could be found in the basin. Meat came from small animals like jackrabbits, squirrels, lizards, gophers, and rats. Grasshoppers and crickets were roasted over the fire when game was scarce.

The Shoshonis learned to travel light, leaving most of their possessions behind when the time came to move on. The dry land taught them to save water. None was used for bathing or cooking, and juices were sucked from berries and roots when no drinking water could be found.

The land also taught them endurance. Some days they were so weak with hunger that they walked unsteadily. There were days when they huddled in the shadow of great rocks to escape the searing heat, while at other times feet and fingers became numb with cold. Life had few gifts to offer them, but the people learned to reach out for the gift of laughter. To the Shoshonis a noble person was the person who could smile in the face of trouble.

The land taught them family closeness. Roaming day after day, the children, parents, and the old ones in each family knew only each other. Each felt strongly the need for all the others. If one person found a few weed seeds, the whole family rejoiced. If you had the good sense to share meat on your day of plenty, someone else would have berries for you on the day of your hunger.

A person's value was not measured by how much was owned, but by how much was shared. The land taught the Shoshonis to share what they had, and in turn they came to respect the land. For the Shoshonis, as for most American Indians, the land was there to be shared by all who needed it. They had no idea of what it meant to own land.

The desert was a tough land that formed a gentle people. Without territory or things of value to defend, the Shoshonis had little reason to wage war. The people who lived in the valley were poor; they were often hungry; but they were a patient people who had learned to walk in peace.

After the people had lived in the basin for many generations, a few Shoshoni families left the desert and moved up into the neighboring mountains. Sacagawea's family were descendants of these mountain or Plateau Indians, known as the North Shoshonis. One of the rivers that flowed through their country, the Snake River, gave them another name, the Snake Indians.

These newcomers found a rugged land of snow-mantled mountains, forests, and lakes. Cold streams fed by melting snow gave pure water for drinking, cooking, and bathing. Their long thirst was at an end.

Life was still tuned to the rhythm of the seasons. Their calendar was based on the ripening of gooseberries or currants, the growth of camas roots, and the movements of game animals. While food had become more plentiful, there were still days of hunger.

Every Shoshoni girl was trained in the art of food-gathering. At first she simply followed her mother, picking up the bulbs dug from the ground. Before long she had learned the names of more than one hundred edible plants and how to judge when they were ready to be gathered. She learned to pull her hand gently along a stem so berries would not be crushed before they bounced into her basket.

Acorns, grass seeds, and piñon nuts were ground into meal on stone slabs. A favorite food was the bulb of the camas lily. In springtime the bright camas blossoms made a mountain meadow look like a great blue lake. Large baskets of yucca fibers, waterproofed with pitch, served as cooking pots. Water was heated to a cooking temperature by dropping hot stones into the baskets.

In the high country the Shoshonis found larger game than the lizards and grasshoppers of the basin. Now they learned to hunt for muledeer, antelope, elk, and bear. They had their first taste of the delicate meat of bighorn sheep and learned to like the flavor of waterfowl.

Fear of disease and death moved with the Shoshonis into the mountains. They dealt with those fears through their shamans, just as they had during the desert years. Although it was more common among the men, some women were also shamans. Shamans received special powers from their guiding spirits to cure disease, which they treated by sucking out the evil spirit, by smoking rituals, or by strenuous dances. Special songs called medicine chants also had power to cure.

The belief in Shamanism was a gift from the past when their ancestors had felt close to the animals. Shoshonis believed that spirits live in animals, giving them magical powers. Animal guardians could appear to someone in a dream, offering help in trouble. For one person the animal might be an eagle; for another, a rabbit or a bear. Each clan had its own totem animal, the protector for the family, and each person had an animal guardian, revealed in youth by a dream. The Great Spirit was the god above all other gods, the supreme one who ruled over all.

A new way of life came to the North Shoshoni people with their discovery of the buffalo. For many years they had stayed in the cool forests of the mountains, hunting antelope, elk, and bear. Then they began to move for brief periods a little way out onto the grassy plains. There they saw great herds of buffalo, their shaggy heads swaying heavily as they grazed on the long grasses. Since one buffalo provided as much food as many muledeer or antelope, it seemed wise to travel to the plains to hunt for these larger animals.

Here the Shoshonis met Indians of the Plains tribes, both in trade and in battle. While each tribe had its own language, communication between tribes for trading purposes was by the sign language, a series of simple hand movements. For example, to say "stream" the right hand, palm down, was moved from right to left in a wavy motion. For "rain" both hands were held breast-high with the fingers pointing down. The same gesture made at eye level meant "to weep."

Speaking with signs, the Shoshonis traded their own beads or beaver pelts for other peoples' buckskin, and so learned new customs from neighboring tribes. Like the Plains Indians, they learned to carry their babies in buckskin cradle-boards, and to use iron kettles instead of cooking baskets. They began to make clothing from tanned buckskin with long fringes for decoration. They learned to paddle across streams in bullboats, bowl-shaped craft of buckskin stretched over willow frames.

The tepee was a portable home used by Plains Indians only for their buffalo hunting trips, but the Shoshoni adopted it as a better shelter for their wandering pattern of life. Three strong timbers lashed together at the top and spread out widely at the base formed a three-sided framework, or tripod. The lashing ended in a long rope tied to a stake inside the tepee to steady it against the wind. Other poles were added for strength, and the whole framework was covered with as many as forty hides.

In the mountains the Shoshonis' only work animals had been dogs, but in the wide-open plains they needed horses for hunting buffalo and for traveling long distances. The spotted Appaloosa horses had been brought to North America by Spanish explorers and bred by the Palouse Indians of Oregon. They were handsomely formed, with lean heads, narrow chests, and sparse tails. In spite of their graceful appearance, they proved to be hardy, dependable animals for the hunt.

The Shoshonis quickly learned great riding skill. With horses they could travel farther, but travel also brought new dangers. The coming of the Shoshonis to buffalo territory had alarmed some Plains Indians, who were afraid that the Shoshonis would spread farther and farther into their hunting lands. By bold raids on their camps, the Plains Indians hoped to drive the Shoshonis back into the mountains. The raiders also carried away fine horses and prisoners to be used as slaves.

Threatened by a common enemy, family groups began to band together for protection in winter camps and summer hunting retreats. Thus the gentle Shoshonis were forced to become more warlike. Their fragile reed arrows were no match for the rifles of the tall Plains warriors, but the Shoshonis were learning to admire daring in their own people.

The Shoshonis learned to "count coups," which was actually a ceremony for boasting. The warrior struck a blow with an axe as he told of each deed of bravery. A coup might be for touching the body of a dead enemy, for stealing a horse from the middle of an enemy camp, or perhaps for striking a wounded buffalo on the rump with a bow. Each warrior's coups were pictured in designs on his tepee or on leg marks for ceremonial dancing. Feathered war bonnets and painted shields with mystical powers of protection were added to their gear.

The Shoshonis also learned how to hide, how to keep silent, and how to approach a stranger with caution. Trust had been needed for survival in the desert and in the mountains, but on the plains there were warlike peoples. Those who trusted too much did not survive.

Sacagawea's people had been changed by moving to the mountains and by meeting the tribes from the Great Plains. The horses and the rifles that the whites brought to the Plains Indians had changed their way of life, and the Plains Indians had changed the Shoshonis. Although the Shoshonis had become more spirited and more comfortable, in their hearts they still carried the teachings of the harsh desert.

CHAPTER II

The Hunt
And The Capture

Sacagawea awakened before dawn on the day she and her family would pack up and leave for the hunt. She heard the muffled voices of her father and her brother Cameahwait getting the horses ready outside the tepee.

Among the mountains many Shoshoni families were awakening at dawn for the hunt. All were getting ready to meet at the Three Forks of the Missouri for their summer retreat.

It was always a day of excitement for Shoshoni children, and thoughts of other hunts, other summers filled their minds. Great slabs of buffalo meat, slowly roasting over the fires, brought an end to long months of hunger. Shoshoni children swam together in the cold river, walked through the forest, and listened as the hunters counted coups and described their adventures.

Soon the tepees were emptied, and the clearing was alive with men and women, laughing children, and barking dogs. Tepees were taken down, and each set of lodge poles was lashed together to form a travois, a dragging device used to carry their belongings from one place to another. A large travois could be dragged by strong work horses, while a smaller one could be hitched to a dog team.

Every travois was neatly packed and horses and dogs hitched to them. Women gently picked up sleepy babies and propped the cradleboards on their shoulders. Some of the Shoshoni mounted trail horses, while others walked beside the travois. The procession moved along a rough trail which followed the high ridge, then wound down to the shady river bottom. Just three days away were the Three Forks, Sacagawea's summer friends, and the excitement of the buffalo hunt.

At Three Forks was a broad, beautiful plain where three rivers merged into one larger river, the Missouri. Edging the plain in every direction were mountains, lightly dusted with snow at the peaks. Swans floated along the river shores and beaver cuttings dotted the wooded islands. Prickly pear cactus grew thickly beside the trail.

Here the Shoshonis were within easy riding distance of the Great Plains, where mighty herds of buffalo could be found. And yet the mountains were close enough to offer a hiding place if an enemy should attack. The warlike Hidatsa people, also known as Minnetaree, had been known to come from the east, searching for horses or for slaves. Only in the mountains could the Shoshonis feel truly safe.

Sacagawea's family was not the first to arrive. Already leather tepees were popping up along the river banks and in the willow groves. Bundles were unloaded from the travois, and the children began to arrange their belongings inside the lodge.

Runners were sent out on the plains to find a buffalo herd. When these scouts came back with news that a herd had been sighted, the other men and older boys mounted everyday trail horses and rode off. Running beside each

The Three Forks of the Missouri River, where the Shoshonis set up their summer hunting camp.

mount was a faster, highly trained buffalo horse.

Sacagawea listened to the hoofbeats dwindling off into silence and then returned to the busy life of the camp with the women and other children. Cameahwait and the other older boys had gone with the hunters to see and to learn. He was quiet and gentle around the tepee and the campfire, but his face lit up with joy as he rode his spotted horse in the hunt. Coming back in mid-afternoon, streaked with sweat, weary, but excited, Cameahwait slid from his horse and led it down to the river. As the horse poked its muzzle into the water, he told Sacagawea the story of the day's hunt.

Sacagawea could almost see the hunting party as it rode up to the buffalo herd. Leading the group were the hunting chief, who gave the orders, and the shaman, who prayed to the guiding spirits for hunting success. The boys rode behind the main body of hunters, watching from a distance.

Nearing the herd, the hunters got into formation on the buffalo horses and waited for the chief's signal to start the chase. They raced across the grassy plain toward the buffalo while they shouted to frighten them into a stampede. Men armed with bows attacked from the right; then those with spears came in from the left, thrusting the spears deep into the buffaloes' shaggy sides.

After the charge the hunters left the wounded buffalo lying where they fell and rode quickly back to where the boys waited with the everyday horses. Then they changed mounts and rode in formation back to camp.

Sacagawea scarcely had time to hear Cameahwait's story before she had to leave with the women to take care of the skinning duties. Using knives of sharpened shinbone or flint, the women cut the meat free of the hide and then sliced it into pieces small enough for the young girls to lift onto the travois. Back in camp the real processing would take place. Some meat would be eaten fresh while other cuts, smoked until they were hard and leathery, could be kept for trail food all year without spoiling.

Every part of the body had some use. Sinews served as bowstrings or lacings. Bones became sled runners, axes, and other tools. Hoofs yielded a kind of glue and the horns were made into arrow points, ladles, and cups.

Early the next morning, Sacagawea and her friends were put to work tanning robes for winter use. Preparing hides for use was hard work, and the girls were glad when they were allowed to leave and go down by the stream to talk. It was peaceful there, with only the sounds of the flowing water, a few bird calls, the low murmur of talk and soft laughter.

Suddenly the crack of rifle fire shattered the summer silence. Sacagawea looked up to see a band of tall, mounted Hidatsa warriors, swooping like hawks into the camp, jerking loose the rawhide ropes with which the Shoshoni horses were tied. She saw the men of her tribe spring up in confusion, reaching for their bows, struggling against the raiders. She saw women grabbing small children by the hand and pushing them toward the woods.

At first Sacagawea was too frightened to move, too startled even to cry out. She looked wildly in all directions for a way to escape. The river! Could she wade through the rocky shoals and escape to the other side?

As she stepped into the icy water the current tugged at her legs, almost pushing her down. Sharp rocks cut her feet. Desperately she tried to push herself forward across the ridge of rocks, but the force of the water was too strong for her.

Then she could hear horses crashing through the brush and splashing into the river. Rough hands grabbed her shoulders, pulling her up out of the water and onto the back of a horse. Sacagawea fought to free herself, but her strength was no match for the Hidatsa warrior. Around her other girls were being snatched from the water and carried away.

Back near the cooking fires, she saw Shoshoni men lying wounded and dying. As the horse galloped out toward the open prairie, she looked back in silent horror at the camp of her people, darkened with smoke.

Sacagawea did not cry out. Her throat was tight, eyes aching with unshed tears. Why had they taken her and the others? Where were they being taken? What would become of them? If there was a chance to escape from these warriors, she was too stunned by fear and sorrow to form a plan. The bruises on her shoulders and throat were proof that they were strong and determined.

For many days the Hidatsa and their Shoshoni captives rode across the prairie, following the Yellowstone River and the great Missouri. Sacagawea felt herself being carried further each day from the Land of the Shining Mountains.

At times the captives were allowed to ride, and at other times they walked. Soon every familiar landmark had been left behind. The prairie rose in rounded hills, and then flattened for long miles—a wavy sea of grass in all directions. Only the river seemed alive and real. Only the river was tied at one end to the land of her people.

CHAPTER III

A New Life
On The Plains

As Sacagawea stood on the bank of the Missouri river in the spring of 1804, she must have longed for the answers she did not know. Was her father one of the men she had seen lying on the ground, felled by rifle fire? What had become of her brothers? Did Cameahwait still live? Had her mother and sister reached safety in the woods?

More than three years had passed since she was brought to the Hidatsa village on the prairies of what is now North Dakota, but still she often thought about her capture and the journey that followed.

She had first seen the village after long weary days of travel. When they had come to the place where the Knife River joins the Missouri, the land had suddenly changed. Where once she had seen only brush and grass and a few scattered cottonwood and willow trees, she now saw straight green rows of corn rustling in the summer wind. These planted fields had been a strange sight to a girl trained to search for scattered wild plants.

Then, high on the bank, she had seen the village. Its grass-covered earthen lodges were like great overturned bowls, a curl of smoke coming from the top of each. The Hidatsa warriors had noticed her shyness and bewilderment,

Unlike the tepees of Sacagawea's people, grass-covered earthen lodges gave the Plains Indians good protection from fierce weather. They were roomy inside, too.

and they motioned to her to climb the bank and go into the village.

A round open area in the center was bordered by rings of the lodges, sturdy shelters partly dug into the ground. The sight of the lodges must have puzzled Sacagawea, because she had seen only simple brush wickiups or leather tepees. Had it not been from the Plains tribes that the Shoshoni had learned to make tepees? She was to learn that the folding tepees were used by the Hidatsa only when moving about on the hunt. Having learned to work the soil, they could settle down in one village, leaving only now and then to hunt. At home the earthen lodges offered better protection from the sun, the cold, and the prairie wind.

For Sacagawea a whole new way of life began that day, though some things in Hidatsa life were familiar to her. The sign language helped her in learning to speak Hidatsa, and so served as a bridge between the Shoshoni and the Hidatsa way. Also, the Shoshonis had borrowed many customs from these buffalo hunters of the plains. Like the Shoshonis they dressed in buckskin. In summer the men wore only breechcloths and moccasins, while the women had calf-length dresses and short leggings.

Sacagawea soon learned that she had been brought to the Hidatsa village to work, and she spent long hours in the fields with the women. The corn, called maize by the Hidatsa, was planted early in the spring by digging a shallow trench with a pointed ash stick and dropping seed into it. In summer the women and girls hoed the fields with the shoulder bone of a buffalo lashed to a wooden handle.

Tender young ears of corn were picked in the summer time, gathered into big baskets, and cooked fresh. Most of the harvest waited until the plants were fully ripe. After husking the ears were laid on a platform to dry, and then beaten with sticks until the kernels flew off. Finally the kernels were tossed around in baskets to get rid of the chaff.

Like everyone else in the villages, Sacagawea must have enjoyed the ceremonial dances and the games. The dancers wore brightly colored costumes and filled the air with the sounds of deer-hoof rattles and double-headed drums. With the other girls and women, she watched the boys play the hoop game in the open space at the center of the village. Leaping like young deer, they tossed a hoop high into the air and caught it with pronged sticks.

The men seemed to enjoy gambling games like the moccasin game. When Sacagawea walked from the river bank into the village a moccasin game was in progress, so she found a place among the women and sat down on the ground to watch. Two teams of three men each played the game, while others sang and beat drums.

The players used four moccasins, together with four pebbles, one of which had a small mark on it. They took turns guessing under which moccasin the marked pebble had been placed, pointing at their guess with a long rod. The losers had to give up something of value to the winners —usually knives, beaver pelts, or beads.

Sacagawea's master was playing in the game, and things were not going well for him. Again and again he guessed wrong, the marked pebble was uncovered, and he was forced to give up his belongings. Finally she saw him talking with Toussaint Charbonneau, the French-Canadian fur trader who lived among the Hidatsa. The other men stood around listening to their conversation. Then some of them began laughing, drums began to beat, and her master walked over to her, pulled her to her feet, and pushed her toward the grinning Charbonneau.

Amid the shouting she understood what had happened. She had been the prize in this game of chance! Her master no longer owned her as a slave girl. She was to be Charbonneau's woman, his wife. Because a marked pebble was found under a certain shoe, her life was to be joined to the life of this bearded, aging fur trader, a man who already had another Indian wife.

Sacagawea knew that the Mandans and the Hidatsa laughed at him, giving him such names as Great Horse From Afar and Forest Bear. Charbonneau had lived in the village for about eight summers, developing a reputation as a slow-witted, clumsy person. He served as an interpreter for traders, and he had learned the sign language and just enough words from each tribal language to communicate with all the Plains tribes. Sacagawea may have been fearful of his rough manner and his hearty laughter, but he was not known for unkindness.

She had no choice. She had not been free to choose when she was torn from the waters of the stream and brought to this village. Neither was she free to choose a husband. Still Sacagawea had lived bravely and with honor. Her family and her childhood name had been taken from her; the Shoshoni marriage promise made for her at her birth had been broken; she had been torn loose from the mountains and the forests and the waterfalls; she had even been called "Charbonneau's woman." One thing they could not take away was her loyalty to her people. Sacagawea was still a Shoshoni.

CHAPTER IV

The White Explorers Come

The Shoshonis had adapted to life on the desert and then to life in the mountains. Sacajawea had learned to adjust to the plains. Now she began to adjust to life in the lodge of Toussaint Charbonneau, the French-Canadian fur trader who had become her husband. She was uncomfortable at first with his loud laughter and his endless talking, but she soon became used to both. He sometimes shouted at her in impatience, but this was as natural to him as the roar of a waterfall. They spoke with each other in the Hidatsa and sign languages.

Now it was autumn, harvest time, and Sacajawea was approaching motherhood. For the young wife it was a time of joy. One cold, windy November day she sat near the doorway of their lodge, lacing moccasins and lining them with dried grass for winter. Suddenly she heard Charbonneau shouting her name.

White warriors had come, many of them, moving up the Missouri from the south in boats, with a team of horses following beside them on the bank. Chiefs from the Mandan village had met some of the white men while hunting. They had gone to the river and invited them to visit their village. White and Mandan chiefs had smoked the pipe together, because these strangers had come in peace. Crowds from all the Mandan and Hidatsa villages were gathering by the river to look at the splendid boats and at the men in dusty blue uniforms. The strange men had come many days' journey from Wood River, Illinois, a short distance up the Mississippi River from Saint Louis.

Sacagawea listened, but did not believe. Now and then a white trader had come to the villages, and she was married to a white man, but a whole band of them! Why had they come so far? Were they also looking for the buffalo which roamed the plains? She joined the women and children who hurried to the river.

Lying at anchor was a big keelboat, a low covered vessel used for hauling freight. It had a small sail and long rows of oars. At each end was a swivel gun, a small cannon which could be swung in all directions in case of attack. Back of the keelboat were two pirogues. These were long, slim dugouts, shaped rather like a canoe, but tapered at the front and squared-off at the tail. Instead of paddles they were rowed with oars. Each pirogue also had a small sail, to be raised only when a strong wind was blowing.

The strangers had set up a camp on the bank with leather, military-style tents. Fluttering from a tall pole was their red, white, and blue flag. Hidatsas and Mandans came close to look as the strangers cooked or worked on their weapons. The Indians gave them gifts of cornmeal and buffalo robes, while the strangers offered looking glasses, tobacco, and armbands in return.

The visitors were looking for a place to set up a winter camp, where they planned to wait until spring before once more following the river westward. Both wood and game were scarce around their temporary camp, so they decided to build a little further downstream in the wooded bottomland. Axes rang for hours each day in the woods, as they chopped down cottonwood trees for the winter camp, now called Fort Mandan. Flocks of ducks passing overhead reminded the workers that winter was near and that shelters must be built quickly.

Two rows of log sheds were joined together at right angles, each row containing four small rooms. The slanting roof formed a loft over each room. As the building continued, Charbonneau came one day to see the white chiefs, offering to serve as their interpreter for the winter dealings with Mandan and Hidatsa Indians. These languages were unknown to them, so the white leaders agreed.

Charbonneau began to learn more about the soldiers, and soon he was able to answer Sacagawea's questions. He told her that President Thomas Jefferson, the great white chief who ruled in a city far to the east, had paid money to Napoleon of France for vast stretches of land where many Indian tribes now lived. The land that the United States bought from France was called the Louisiana Territory.

Fort Mandan, the winter camp that the white strangers built, looked just like this reconstruction.

But Mr. Jefferson had never seen the country that he now claimed. Was it good land to live in? What plants and animals were found there? Were there new areas for the fur trade? What of the languages and customs of the Indian tribes? President Jefferson had heard stories about a Northwest Passage through the mountains, an easy one-day's portage from the source of the Missouri to the Columbia River. The Columbia could be followed to the Pacific Ocean, known to most Indian tribes as the Great Waters Where the Sun Sets.

Sea otters from the Pacific Coast had long been valuable in foreign trade. Until this time, however, it had been necessary to send big sailing ships all the way around Cape Horn at the tip of South America and up the west coast to the mouth of the Columbia in order to get them. The United States did have some claim on the Pacific shoreline, but had been unable to reach it overland without invading the area claimed by the French. The Louisiana Purchase cleared the way to go by land. An overland river route along the Missouri and Columbia rivers would be a far cheaper, safer way to carry the Pacific Coast furs. Was there such a way?

To answer his questions the president had asked two friends, Captains Meriwether Lewis and William Clark, to form a party known as the Corps of Discovery. Jefferson wanted them to reveal the secrets of the Louisiana Purchase lands. They would draw maps, gather samples of plants and wildlife, and study the ways of the Indian tribes. Lewis and Clark were asked to discover the safest, most direct pathway to the ocean.

In his work as interpreter, Charbonneau helped the young captains to understand the Mandan and the Hidatsa people.

Meriwether Lewis (left) and William Clark (right), leaders of the Corps of Discovery.

The Mandans, he pointed out, were a peaceful people, and had never traveled far from their own villages. Lewis and Clark might learn more about the lands to the west by speaking with the Hidatsa. Their daring raids had carried them to the very edge of the Rockies.

As he worked with the explorers, Charbonneau seemed to catch their spirit of adventure. He offered to sign on for the expedition, and the captains agreed. Charbonneau was invited to move into the fort and help with preparations.

Horses would be needed for the mountain crossing, according to Hidatsa reports. Perhaps these could be bought from the Shoshoni people. But they could not bargain with Shoshonis because most interpreters did not understand their language. It was then Charbonneau told the captains that he had a Shoshoni wife. Maybe she would help them in dealing with the people of her tribe. Sacagawea could become a part of the Corps of Discovery.

At first the captains were not sure that she should join the expedition, because she was about to give birth, and there would be hardships along the trail. Charbonneau reminded them that the Shoshonis were known for their endurance. Also, when they met with new tribes, a woman might be seen as a token of peace. Lewis and Clark decided that Charbonneau should bring his Shoshoni wife to Fort Mandan for the winter, and in the spring she would go with the Corps of Discovery on its expedition. Sacagawea appeared to receive the news calmly, but later events leave little doubt about her deep longings. At last she would return to the land of her people!

While the men were busy hunting or getting their gear in order, the two young captains were gathering and recording information. Captain Lewis, a quiet, handsome man, spent much of the time alone at his desk. He was recording information about plants and animals that he had found on the journey. Captain Clark, cheerful and friendly, was trained in map-making and showed great skill in dealing with the Indians who came to the fort. He soon became known as the "white man whose tongue is straight."

Almost daily Indians from the village visited the fort. Captain Lewis questioned the visitors about life in the Mandan area, filling notebooks which would be sent back to Saint Louis in the spring. Captain Clark, meanwhile, questioned the Hidatsas about the land that still lay ahead.

Sketching rough maps on strips of hide or on the dirt floor, the Hidatsa hunters traced a route westward, describing distances in terms of "three days' travel" or "so many sleeps." It became clear that the explorers could find their way to the Rockies and to the horses needed for mountain travel only if they could follow the Missouri River to its source. They must stay with the "true Missouri" and not turn off at one of its tributaries, even though the tributary might appear to be the main branch of the Missouri at that point. The captains listened closely and wrote down such names as the Yellowstone and the River Which Scolds at All Others (later renamed the Milk River). They would know they had followed the "true Missouri" when they came to a spectacular waterfall, the Great Falls of the Missouri.

The firing of Fort Mandan's swivel guns began a day of Christmas celebration. Sacagawea knew nothing about Christmas, but she was told it was the explorers' "Big Medicine Day," when they honored their guardian spirit. She watched as the explorers danced to the music of fiddle, tambourine, and horn.

As the weeks went by, Sacagawea knew that soon her child would be born. She spent most of her time sewing little moccasins, and making cornhusk dolls and a buckskin cradleboard for the baby. On February 11 the birth pangs began. Lying on a buffalo robe surrounded by rough and bearded men, Sacagawea bore in silence the pain of a long and difficult labor.

One of the men suggested to Captain Lewis that a snake's rattle could be given to her to quicken the labor. Captain Lewis brought him a rattle, which was broken up, mixed with water, and poured down Sacagawea's throat. Within ten minutes Jean Baptiste Charbonneau was born, and the young mother gathered him into her arms. The captains called him "Pomp," an Indian word for "little chief," and from that day he was Pomp or Pompy to everyone.

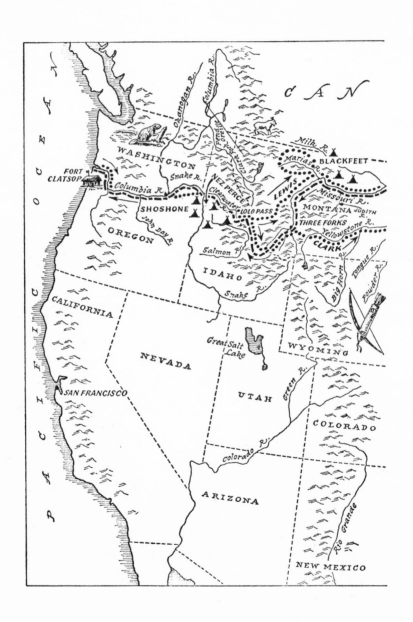

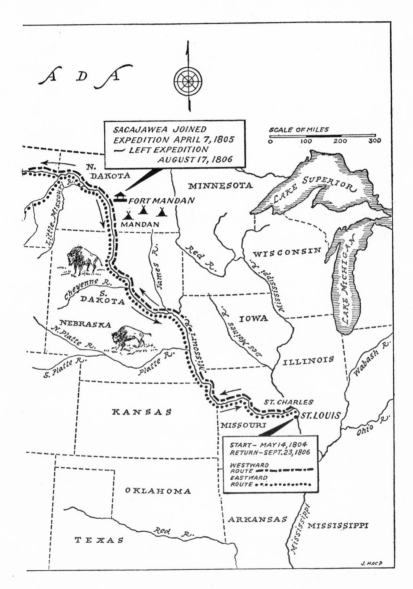

Map of the Lewis and Clark expedition route.

Sacagawea was exhausted from the birth struggle, but proud of her bright-eyed Pompy. Her young body easily recovered its strength. With each day she was able to do more work and to prepare herself for the journey.

In March, when the snow on the roof had begun to soften, it was time to think of boats for the journey. The pirogues and the keelboat were pried from the ice and pulled up on land to repair the seams. The keelboat would be too large for the shallow upper Missouri, so they would send it back to Saint Louis. They made six dugout canoes from cottonwood to replace it.

The explorers had to plan with great care what they would carry into the unknown land between them and the Pacific Ocean. Survival would depend on their own skills, the tools and supplies they could carry along, and the help that might be given by the Indians they would meet along the way. They would need clothing and moccasins to replace those that would wear out. Needles and thread would be required for mending, while simple clothing would have to be made from skins along the way. They would need flints, lead, ammunition, and rifles for hunting and to defend themselves from attack. Blacksmith tools would be useful for mending equipment and for shoeing horses.

They could carry some dried foods, but they would try to "live off the land," hunting game animals, fishing, and gathering wild plants and berries. For the explorers, "living off the land" would be different from the Shoshoni way of life. They tried to keep their equipment down to a manageable size, but they ended up taking such luxuries as kegs of spirits, rolls of tobacco, musical instruments, and lap desks for the captains.

Much of the load was for trade with the Indians. They packed such things as painted beads, calico shirts, fish hooks, American flags, and medals stamped with the president's picture. Their doubts about how the Indian tribes would receive them could be seen in the pipe-tomahawks they packed. At one end of a short handle was a tomahawk, an instrument of war. At the other end was a pipe of peace.

For her family, Sacagawea packed the skin envelopes called parfleches with tunics, buckskin leggings, beads, lacing, awls, and knives. Remembering her days of hunger in Shoshoni country, she tucked in bits of sugar for Pompy and pieces of dried bread for herself.

The river ice broke up with such force that it almost destroyed the new dugout canoes. After the long winter the explorers eagerly looked forward to the coming journey, and every evening they danced to the tune of Private Cruzatte's violin. Fort Mandan would soon be left behind, and the Corps of Discovery would follow the river to Shoshoni country and beyond.

CHAPTER V

The Long
Journey Begins

Sacagawea stuffed a little more soft, dry grass into Pompy's cradleboard, put the child into it, and tied the rawhide thongs. Her eyes swept the room that had sheltered her through the winter, now stripped of the buffalo robes and the hunting and cooking gear. The last fire was dying on the hearth as she stepped outside.

The ground under her moccasins was spongy and damp from the melting snow. Tender new buds dotted the cottonwoods. For several days Lewis and Clark had seen swans and wild geese flying northeastward in the evening. The Hidatsas had been leaping across the ice cakes to catch the buffalo floating downstream. Soon the river would be ice-free and ready. The captains had taken charge of the final packing, carefully separating the maps, papers, and wildlife specimens that would be sent back to President Jefferson from the provisions that would go farther up the Missouri with their Corps of Discovery.

Now it was April 7, 1805. Today they would say good-bye to the Mandans and Hidatsas, who watched from the banks of the river. It would also be a day of parting for six American soldiers and two French traders, who would return to Saint Louis with the keelboat and two canoes. The main

Pompy would travel in a cradleboard like this Nez Percé baby.

party of the Corps of Discovery—Captains Lewis and Clark, Sacagawea, Pompy, Charbonneau and another interpreter, three sergeants, twenty-three privates, and a black slave named York—would follow the Missouri westward in the two long pirogues and six dugout canoes.

This day in the springtime of Sacagawea's seventeenth year was another round in the strange moccasin game of her life. Chance had placed the Shoshonis at Three Forks when the Hidatsa warriors had raided, leading to the long years away from her people. Chance had joined her to her husband. By chance she had met the white captains, Lewis and Clark, and now chance had brought her to the dawn of this long journey.

Shadows were lengthening into late afternoon when the big keelboat and two canoes began to move back down the Missouri toward Saint Louis. Almost at the same time, the six dugout canoes and two pirogues of the westbound party pushed away from the shoreline and started up the river.

The men were in good spirits—talking, laughing, waving at the Indians along the banks. Sacagawea began the journey more quietly. No sign of excitement showed on her face, and her voice was calm. Only months later would the others realize the depth of her feeling as she started the journey.

Sacagawea took her turn with the others, sometimes paddling in one of the boats, often walking along the shore. The world of the plains seemed to flow by. Flocks of geese fed in the young grass, while sparrow hawks wheeled across the sky. Patches of juniper spread along the sides of the hills. Maple trees were budding and plum bushes were in bloom, but winter was not quite over. Once in a while snow would sift down briefly on a land that had already felt the touch of spring.

At Fort Mandan Sacagawea became acquainted with the military life of the Americans. She had grown used to the uniforms, the salutes, the sentinels, the commands, and had learned the names of the thirty men whom her family had joined. As the real work of the expedition began, she came to know each person as an individual. Each one had been chosen for the skills that would help the Corps of Discovery as a whole.

Captain Lewis was a brave and thoughtful leader who enjoyed walking alone out on the prairie, studying the animals or gathering bits of plant life. It was he who learned to chart their route by the stars. Captain Lewis also served as doctor for the expedition, giving out medicines from his small leather bag. Sacagawea learned that Captain Clark's talents as mapmaker and peacemaker were equalled by his leadership skills.

Private Cruzatte, whose violin music had delighted her at Fort Mandan parties, was experienced in river travel. Sergeant Gass was a carpenter, and Private Shields was an expert gunsmith. Drewyer served as an interpreter, but he was also an able hunter. The black man, York, worked as Captain Clark's personal servant, and he provided entertainment for the whole Corps with his story-telling. Sergeant Ordway became a capable commander whenever the captains were not around. John Colter, from the Kentucky woods, had been chosen for hunting skills, and in a single day he bagged an elk, three deer, a wolf, and five turkeys. Charbonneau proved to be a surprisingly good trail cook.

Even Scannon, Captain Clark's big, black, Newfoundland dog, had his chores. An alert watchdog, he frightened away animals who wandered into camp during the night. He also helped with Pompy, lying like a faithful guardian beside the baby's cradleboard.

Sacagawea cheerfully kept pace along the trail, moving with a light, firm step. Food-gathering skills from her Shoshoni childhood proved useful again and again. Just two days from Fort Mandan, when they had halted for dinner, she sharpened a digger stick and began to poke around in small piles of driftwood. She uncovered a good supply of wild artichokes, buried there by mice.

Day after day Sacagawea walked along the shore or rode in a canoe with the others, but in a sense she made the journey alone. Not even the child on her shoulders shared her experience. No one else could share her dream of home-coming.

Evenings around the campfire were a pleasant time. After supper the men would often throw quoits, a game in which they tossed rope rings at stakes. Sometimes they danced to the music of violin and Jew's harp. The captains and several of the others faithfully wrote down each day's events in their journals by the dim light of the fire. Sacagawea sat cross-legged on the ground, mending buckskins and watching over Pompy.

For several days they passed through prairie country like one large grassy pasture. Gentle herds of buffalo, elk, and antelope gazed at them curiously, sometimes following the men who walked on shore. Deer peered shyly from the brush.

By late April they had reached the woodlands at the mouth of the Yellowstone River. Happy to have arrived at this first important landmark, they celebrated with music, dancing, and a small ration of spirits.

May 14 brought troubles to the expedition. Six of the hunters wounded a brown grizzly. Crazed by pain, the bear charged and chased them along the bank. The men plunged into the river, and others in the party were able to kill the bear with eight shots.

After sunset that evening the white pirogue was almost destroyed. The sail had been raised to take advantage of a brisk wind. Steering was Charbonneau, a timid and clumsy river pilot. A sudden squall struck the boat at an angle, ripping the brace of the sail from the man who held it, and the boat tipped over on its side. Charbonneau had never learned to swim. He cried out to God in terror and dropped the rudder. Cruzatte, in the bow, threatened to shoot him if he did not take hold of the rudder and do his duty. A trembling Charbonneau obeyed.

Meanwhile Sacagawea, balancing the baby on her back, calmly reached far out over the side and grabbed the valuable cargo that had fallen overboard. After the pirogue had been dragged to shore and bailed out with kettles, the rescued articles were spread out on the ground to dry. By her quick thinking Sacagawea had saved many things of value to the expedition. She had rescued instruments for navigation, scientific books needed by the captains for their work, and trading goods needed to make peaceful contacts with Indians they would meet along the way.

Almost every day the travelers reached some new tributary of the Missouri. They remembered maps drawn on skins or in the earth by Hidatsa warriors back at Fort Mandan. As each river was identified by its Hidatsa name, they could feel confident that they were on the right track. When they came to a river with water the tan color of milky tea, they named it the Milk River. This was the river known to the Hidatsas as "The River Which Scolds At All Others." Small, unnamed streams were given new names by Lewis and Clark. When a lively, clear-running river was named for Sacagawea, she accepted the honor with shy pleasure.

Another stream was called Blowing Fly Creek for the hordes of flies that swarmed over their meat. Judith's River was named for a friend of Captain Clark, Julia Hancock of Virginia.

In the high country near the mouth of Judith's river, they found the remains of a large Indian camp that had been deserted a short time before. All over the hills were the scattered ashes of cooking fires where tepees had stood. A child's ball and a moccasin found on the site were brought to Sacagawea. She looked at them carefully, then shook her head. They were not Shoshonis.

In early June the party came to a branching of the river that gave them a problem. Which of the branches was the "true Missouri?" Was it the one that seemed to come from the north, or was it the branch that flowed from the southwest? Most of the Corps were sure that the northern branch was the Missouri. It looked like the river they had followed all the way from the Mississippi, broad and thick with mud. The captains, on the other hand, wanted to follow the southern branch, a clear, swift-running stream with a rock and gravel bed. They reasoned that the Missouri had its source in the mountains and that a mountain stream would be swift and clear.

A wrong decision could be a costly mistake. Already they could see snow-topped mountains in the distance. Even if they should find the "Northwest Passage," crossing the mountains in winter would be a risky business. If they should turn up the wrong river, it could waste precious weeks of summer travel time. The captains decided that a camp should be set up for a few days at the fork of the rivers. Small exploring parties would go up each of the branches and decide which fork led to the Great Falls described by the Hidatsas, and from there to Shoshoni country.

Clearly it was a good time to pause. Those not in the exploring parties could spend their time dressing skins for clothing. Uniforms had fallen to shreds, and buckskin clothing had to be made to replace them. Moccasins had been so cut by the rocky trails that they had been thrown away, and the men could barely walk on their bruised feet. Many of them were exhausted from towing the boats free from sandbars or sloshing through cold water up to their armpits. Poor diet and muddy water caused diarrhea and nausea, while chilling rains brought raging fever.

Lewis was so sure that the muddy northern branch could not be the Missouri that he named it Maria's River, after his cousin, Maria Wood. Nevertheless, he agreed to take a party up this river while Captain Clark explored the southern branch. The Lewis party found out that the northern branch flowed through a picture book country of beautiful birds, wild roses, and herds of game animals, but both he and Clark were still convinced that the southern branch was the Missouri. To find out for sure, they decided that Lewis would take four men and follow the southern branch on foot in search of the Great Falls.

Lewis and a small land party pushed up into the rolling hills and across a level plain. Suddenly he heard the distant sound of falling water and saw spray rising above the horizon. He followed the sound of roaring water until he stood on a pile of rocks and looked in wonder at the water cascading over huge bluffs, nine hundred feet wide and eighty feet high. In some places the water fell in great sheets, while at other points it was broken by rocks into glittering spray. He had reached the Great Falls of the Missouri River. Back at camp, he reported that there was no way to pass this point by water. They would have to organize a portage around the falls, but they had followed the "true Missouri."

Captain Lewis learned that Sacagawea had become ill during his absence. The young woman who had met all the hardships of the journey now lay sick in the covered part of the white pirogue, shaded from the July heat. She was gripped by sharp pains, weak, and exhausted. Her pulse was irregular, and her fingers twitched. Captain Clark had tried medicines and had bled her, but she was no better.

The white explorers were worried. They had grown fond of this brave Shoshoni woman, and she had been useful to them in finding roots, sewing buckskin, and pointing out the landmarks along the way. Now, just when they

The expedition could not go over the Great Falls of the Missouri in dugout canoes.

needed her most, on the very edge of Shoshoni country, she lay close to death.

Finally, in desperation, Captain Lewis had mineral water brought from a nearby sulphur spring and poured it down her throat. Within minutes Sacagawea began to perspire, and her pulse grew stronger. The crisis had passed.

The captains decided that the Maria's River camp would be a good place to leave the large red pirogue and some of the provisions to lighten the load for the portage around the falls and for travel through the mountains. The men dug deep, bottle-shaped holes called caches in the ground and filled them with salt, tools, powder, and lead. Signs of the digging were removed. They dragged the pirogue up on an island, tied it to trees, and covered it with brush.

To move the six dugouts around the falls, they built makeshift wagons. The mast of the white pirogue was cut up for axles and rounds were sliced from a huge cotton-wood tree to form wheels.

The eighteen-mile portage around the Great Falls was an eleven-day struggle. The explorers limped in thin moccasins over needle-sharp ground covered with buffalo tracks and prickly pear cactus, shoving the two heavy, clumsy carts. Axles cracked and wagon tongues broke, so new ones had to be made from willow trees. In a stiff breeze the men hoisted a sail on one of the canoes and the wind helped carry it along on the wagon wheels.

One day a sudden storm pelted the party with huge, bouncing hailstones. Water filled runoff channels, almost sweeping Captain Clark, Sacagawea, and Pompy away in a flash flood. They found shelter under a rock shelf and watched a wall of water moving down the creek. Pushing the mother and baby ahead of him, Captain Clark scrambled up the hill to safety just before they would have been swept away.

After they had completed the exhausting portage, they built two canoes and moved up the river, which was narrow and crowded with islands. At a place where the Missouri loops like a rattlesnake, huge rocks hung out over the banks and pressed the river into a narrow channel. Captain Lewis marvelled at the scene and called it the "Gates of the Rocky Mountains."

Time had been lost in the portage, and the explorers were impatient to find the Shoshonis. Each day they found new signs that the Shoshonis were near, including many small, deserted camps among the hills. Sacagawea pointed out remains of willow shelters and trees that had been stripped of bark, explaining that the Shoshonis used the soft underpart of the wood for food. One morning they saw smoke rising in the distance. They guessed that the Shoshonis might have seen their party and set the prairie afire to warn other families that Blackfeet or Hidatsa warriors might be near.

In a green valley Sacagawea identified White Earth Creek, where her people used to gather earth for their paint. The Three Forks of the Missouri were near. For Sacagawea and for the Corps of Discovery, it was a time of hope. Soon they would set foot in the land of her people, the Land of the Shining Mountains.

CHAPTER VI

Reunion

Every day brought fresh signs that the Shoshonis were near, creating new hope that contact could be made. Sacagawea rode in the river party with Lewis, while Captain Clark and a few others moved ahead by land, scouting for signs of the Shoshonis. The Rocky Mountains crowded in close to the river like tall, rugged giants, and Captain Lewis was worried. They might be headed toward savage rapids or waterfalls. Could the river possibly run through these mountains without suddenly tossing their canoes into some wild, unexpected danger? Sacagawea assured him that the river would not suddenly change. There would be a strong and rapid flow, but no waterfalls that could wreck the canoes.

Misery followed them up the river. Shoulders ached from poling canoes between rocks. Cactus needles pierced their feet, and barbed seeds poked through their leggings. Each evening Sacagawea huddled close to the fire, protecting Pompy from the mosquitoes and gnats that swarmed around his head. They slept under mosquito biers, gauzy netting stretched over wooden frames.

On the morning of July 27, the river route opened suddenly on a beautiful stretch of plains and meadows surrounded by distant high mountains. Sacagawea grew silent and her body became tense. Her eyes moved quickly from water to shore, and then off to the forest that covered the mountain slopes. Quietly she identified this as the place of the Hidatsa raid five summers before. She pointed to the rocky shoals in the middle of the river where she had been pulled up on the horse of the Hidatsa warrior. No word from her could possibly explain the mixture of feelings that almost overwhelmed her. No word from these white men could take away the painful memory of violence. No word from them could possibly add to the joy of her return.

While his party halted for breakfast, Lewis climbed a limestone cliff to get a better view of the Three Forks. He chose the southwest fork as the most promising. When he returned, he found a note from Captain Clark asking them to set up camp there. Canoes were unloaded, the baggage stowed away, and some men were permitted to hunt.

It was almost evening by the time Captain Clark arrived —ill, flushed with fever, and exhausted. There could be no more travel until he recovered.

Together the captains studied the three swift-running forks of the river. No one branch seemed better than the others, so they could call none of them the "true Missouri." The southwest fork, which they decided to follow, they named for President Jefferson. The others were named for Madison and Gallatin, two cabinet officers.

When Captain Clark felt better, exploring parties were sent out in the area around Three Forks. Beginning at dawn and continuing until dark, they paddled among the islands for a distance up the Jefferson, and then marched through the tall grass of the high plain. Always their purpose was the same, to make contact with the Shoshonis.

Captain Lewis and a small party now scouted ahead of

the boats. With every day river travel became more difficult. They were battling tricky currents, wading through
cold water, dragging heavy canoes, and stumbling along the
banks. Soon they must find horses or give up hope.

Sacagawea felt sure that a band of her people would soon
be found. Digging back into childhood memories of Shoshoni customs, she prepared the captains for the meeting to
come. Somehow the gentle Shoshonis must receive a signal
that the Corps of Discovery was on an errand of peace. One
moment of panic could crush her dream in another bloody
burst of violence.

Dressed in buckskin, their faces browned leathery by the
sun, the explorers might easily be mistaken for Hidatsa or
Blackfeet warriors. Sacagawea taught them to say the words,
"Ta-ba-bone," meaning, "I am a white man."

She said that the offering of gifts would be seen as a
friendly gesture and that blue beads would be especially
prized. Raising a blanket high in the air and then spreading
it on the ground, she told them, was a Shoshoni sign for
friendship. Another sign was smearing paint on the cheeks.
The captains also learned the pipe-smoking ritual used in
councils of peace.

It was the tenth of August when Lewis and three of his
men went to explore an Indian trail pointed out by Sacagawea. She had recognized the place where her family's
tepee had once stood as the beginning of a trail through the
mountains. Lewis left a note telling Captain Clark that they
were determined to find the Shoshonis and asking his party
to follow them. They followed the trail up a narrow creek
until they reached a lovely valley Lewis named Shoshoni
Cove where they spent the night.

Walking along the creek with McNeal the next morning, Lewis saw an Indian riding toward them in the distance. He studied the rider through his glass and noted that his dress was slightly different from that of the Plains Indians. There was no saddle on his horse and only a thin string under its jaw served as a bridle. His only weapons were a bow and a quiver of arrows.

Captain Lewis braced himself to control his excitement. At last a Shoshoni had crossed his path! Somehow this one Indian must be shown that they were white people and had come in peace. Lewis loosened a blanket from his pack. Holding it by two corners, he threw it up in the air, and then spread it on the ground three times. The Shoshoni paused. Captain Lewis pulled some beads and a looking glass from his pack. Leaving his gun and pouch with McNeal, he slowly walked forward, repeating the words taught to him by Sacagawea, "Ta-ba-bone." He stripped his sleeve up his arm to show the color of his skin.

Shields and Drewyer had come into sight and began moving toward them. The Shoshoni stiffened, glancing suspiciously over his shoulder at the men. Captain Lewis tried to signal them to stop, but Shields pressed forward. The rider suddenly turned his horse about, leaped across the creek, and disappeared into the willow brush.

Angry with Shields and disappointed, Lewis began to follow the horse's tracks up into the hills. Many Shoshonis might be camping up there, watching every move of the strangers. Three days later the Lewis party saw two women, a man, and some dogs watching them in the distance. The captain laid down his pack, picked up the flag, and shouted "Ta-ba-bone" as he walked toward them. The Indians disappeared over the hill before he could reach them.

Minutes later, in a steep ravine, the white men suddenly met three Shoshonis, just thirty paces away. A young woman fled, but an old woman and a girl just stood there, frozen by fear. They sank to the ground, bowing their heads, ready for death. Captain Lewis gently took the old woman's hand and pulled her to her feet, saying "Ta-ba-bone," as he pushed up his sleeve. He offered her a handful of moccasin awls, beads, and looking glasses. She breathed a long sigh and smiled and reached out for the trading gifts.

Using sign language, Drewyer asked them to call the young woman back. After they had given her some gifts, the explorers smeared a bright red paint on the cheeks of all three as a sign of friendship and asked to be taken to their camp. The women walked in front of them as they marched down the trail. Suddenly a large group of Shoshoni warriors came toward them at full speed, mounted on handsome spotted horses. Once again Captain Lewis went through the signs of friendship—laying down his rifle, waving the flag, showing his white skin.

The chief and two others talked with the women, nodding solemnly as they saw the gifts, and then they embraced Captain Lewis. Placing an arm over his shoulder and clasping his back, they rubbed cheeks with him, shouting, "A-hí-e! a-hí-e!" meaning, "I am much rejoiced."

Soon all the explorers were being hugged and smeared with paint. Captain Lewis offered the Shoshonis a folded flag and blue beads, and he persuaded the chief to lead them to his camp for further talks. At the camp they were led to a tepee which had been prepared and were seated on green boughs covered with antelope hide. In a circle at the center, grass had been pulled up and a fire lit. They were told to remove their moccasins, and a more elaborate ceremony began.

The chief pointed his pipe stem to the four points of the heavens, from east to north. He held the pipe out to Captain Lewis, but when he reached for it the chief drew it back and repeated the ceremony three times. Next he passed it to the captain and his men, and then to his own warriors.

Lewis was told in sign language that it would be impossible to go all the way through the mountains along the river that flowed through the camp. He also learned that this band had recently been attacked by enemy warriors, that twenty Shoshonis had been captured, and that they had lost tepees and many horses.

The Shoshonis had no meat, but they shared chokeberry cakes and made the strangers feel welcome. At sunset the dancing began. The four explorers were entertained far into the night and fell asleep with the music still sounding through the camp.

The following day the Shoshoni chief agreed to travel with Lewis to rejoin the main party of the Corps of Discovery and return with supplies for trading talks. Captain Lewis told the Shoshonis in sign language that at Shoshoni Cove they would be joined by another white chief and his people. The chief agreed to go with the white explorers at the next sunrise.

Lewis awakened at dawn eager to set out for Shoshoni Cove, but something had gone wrong. He found the chief waving his arms and looking stern and angry as he spoke to his people. Most of the warriors eyed the explorers suspiciously.

Lewis smoked a pipe like this one, held by the famous Shoshoni chief, Washakie.

Sensing their fear and rebellion, Captain Lewis decided he must appeal to their pride. Speaking in sign language, he said he hoped there might be some among them who were not afraid of death, and that they would decide to go along to discover the truth of his claims. To show his bravery, the tall Shoshoni chief announced that he was not afraid to die and that he hoped others would mount their horses and prove their courage. A few of the men listened to his words and slowly mounted their horses. Soon many others joined them, including three women, and started down the trail.

Although the threat of open rebellion had passed, traces of fear remained. Lewis's men were asked to dress like Indians as a sign that they were casting their lot with the Shoshonis. For the two days that they rode through the forest, each group suspected the other.

When they reached Shoshoni Cove, Captain Clark's party had not yet come. Captain Lewis looked at the Shoshonis, their faces still full of distrust. The other white chief would come soon, Lewis insisted, and a Shoshoni woman and her child would be with them.

As proof of their peaceful intentions, he and his men handed their rifles and pouches to the Shoshoni chief. Captain Lewis promised that if his words were not true, the chief was free to shoot him. The chief accepted the arms, and they waited in uneasy silence.

The note! Suddenly Lewis remembered the note he had left for Captain Clark. Privately he ordered Drewyer to slip away, find the note, and bring it back to him without saying a word. He read from the paper, pretending it was from Captain Clark, and told the chief that the Clark party was just below the mountains. Perhaps one explorer and one Shoshoni should be sent to check his story. A young warrior offered to go with Drewyer on the mission. Captain Lewis watched them go, afraid that the Clark party would have to come soon or all would be lost. All that night Lewis slept with an armed Shoshoni chief standing guard over him.

Meanwhile Clark's river party was finally approaching Shoshoni Cove after a difficult passage. The water was shallow and swift, and their legs ached with cold. Sacagawea and Charbonneau were on land, picking berries as they walked, while Captain Clark limped behind them through tall, dew-covered grass.

Suddenly Sacagawea burst into a wild and joyous dance. She jumped about, waving her arms and pointing to two mounted men coming toward them. She stuck her fingers into her mouth and sucked them—sign language for "These are my people." As Sacagawea drew closer to the men, she recognized one of them as Drewyer, dressed as a Shoshoni. A note that he handed to Captain Clark explained Lewis' situation and urged them to come quickly to Shoshoni Cove.

Many Shoshonis welcomed them as they arrived. A young woman made her way through the crowd toward Sacagawea. Each studied the other for a moment; then they wrapped their arms around each other in a strong embrace. This was Sacagawea's childhood friend, a girl who had been captured with her and had suffered with her on the long journey across the plains. She had somehow escaped from the Hidatsa and found her way back to her people.

Then a Shoshoni man stepped forward and spoke his name, while Sacagawea stood in troubled silence. Many years before she had been promised to this man as his future bride. She gestured toward Charbonneau, and Pompy. The Shoshoni warrior understood and gave up the claim that he had held since childhood.

Captain Clark had exchanged embraces with the Shoshoni leaders and was led to a willow shelter. As an honored guest he was seated on a white robe, while the chief tied six small, pearl-like shells in his hair. Moccasins were removed as a proof of sincerity, and the smoking ceremony began.

Sacagawea was brought into the council shelter. The work for which she had made the journey would now begin. Eyes lowered, she entered, sat down, and acted as an interpreter for Captain Clark. The Shoshoni chief spoke in reply. She listened closely to his words and studied his strong, kindly face. Then she leaped to her feet and embraced him. Cameahwait! Alive! The tall brother of her childhood had survived to become chief of this Shoshoni band.

When the council began again, Sacagawea spoke for the captains and Cameahwait, but now and then the words seemed to choke her and she was overcome by tears. At the close of the meeting Cameahwait confirmed what she had feared. All of her family were dead except for another brother and her sister's son.

The following morning Cameahwait, Sacagawea, Captain Clark, eleven explorers, and most of the Shoshonis left to travel to the Shoshoni camp on the Lemhi River. Captain Lewis and the rest of the explorers stayed behind at Shoshoni Cove to work with the baggage, sorting it and placing some in caches. After four days Cameahwait returned to Shoshoni Cove with horses, while Clark's party continued on to explore the Salmon River. Then Lewis, Cameahwait, and the other explorers and Shoshonis crossed the Lemhi Pass and joined Sacagawea at the camp on the Lemhi River. Clark sent back a note saying that the Salmon was too dangerous to travel on, and he soon returned to the Lemhi River camp.

Sacagawea was busy moving back and forth from the

explorers to the Shoshonis, helping each to understand the ways of the other. They worked together, smoked together, and shared what little food they had. The explorers grew to admire the cheerful, clever Shoshonis, who had much to teach them about the art of survival.

Sacagawea watched as Cameahwait drew maps of possible routes to the sea. He scratched lines to represent rivers and piled up sand to show the mountain ranges. The explorers learned that the Rockies could be crossed only if they knew the way through the right passes, narrow gaps between the high mountain peaks. To begin the crossing they would follow the Lemhi River, which ran through camp westward toward the Lost Trail Pass. In this part of the journey they would be crossing the Continental Divide, the high dividing point of the American continent from which all rivers flow in opposite directions. Some flow westward to the ocean, while others flow eastward across the plains.

Cameahwait warned that they would not be able to move from the Lemhi into the Salmon River, which flowed straight west through a deep, narrow gorge. The Salmon's rapids would be too rough for canoes, and its rocky shores would be too rugged for the horses. Captain Clark's scouting party had reached the Salmon, and he knew it would not be navigable.

An old and wise Shoshoni guide was called in to describe the two choices of overland routes. He warned against the bleak and dangerous southern route. It would mean ten days of travel through a great desert wilderness, where neither game nor water would be found. The northern route would also be exhausting and dangerous. In the Bitterroot River valley, game would be scarce, and far to the north they would have to cross the Bitterroot Range of the Rocky Mountains. Their best hope would be to cross along the Lolo Trail, used by the Nez Percés when they made their summer hunting trips from their river villages west of the mountains into the buffalo country of the Montana plains.

Captain Lewis looked down at the sand map at his feet and decided quickly. The northern route would be the only choice. If the Nez Percés could make it with their women and children, the explorers could make it, too.

Horse trading with the Shoshonis went slowly at first. A few horses were exchanged for trading goods—gingham shirts, uniforms, Jefferson medals, or tobacco. However, it was the promise of protection from the Hidatsa and their other enemies that brought a real response, the promise of twenty horses and several guides. The agreement was made, and Captain Lewis ordered a night of fiddle music and dancing to celebrate.

As the time grew near for moving on, one unanswered question remained. Would Sacagawea leave the land of her people, or would she and Pompy stay with Cameahwait and the Shoshonis? Here she could be safe and happy. Perhaps her place was with her people.

And yet, in another sense, the Corps of Discovery had become "her people." Captains Lewis and Clark were kindly men who had great respect for the Indian way of life. Like the Shoshonis they were able to learn from the land, and she trusted them. Sacagawea decided not to say good-bye to her husband and the other explorers at this halfway point. She would go with them all the way to the Great Waters, to the Pacific Ocean.

CHAPTER VII

To The Great Waters

Tears stung Sacagawea's eyes as she said good-bye to her people and to Cameahwait. On August 27 she and Pompy left the Shoshonis and moved on with the Corps of Discovery. They had bought twenty-nine horses for packing —"and to eat, if necessary," Captain Clark added grimly.

Guided by Cameahwait's instructions and Clark's scouting reports, they would follow the Lemhi River to its junction with the Salmon, and then turn up a canyon northwestward through the Bitterroot Valley to the Lolo Trail. There they hoped to get help from the Nez Percé people for the dangerous mountain crossing. Starting out with them were an old Shoshoni guide named Toby, his son, and five other Shoshonis. By September 1 all had turned back except for Toby and his son.

The mountain trail through the Lost Trail Pass over the Continental Divide was a hard struggle. Toby showed them the way as they labored up and down rocky hillsides, often cutting new trails through scratchy thickets. Horses lost their footing on the steep slopes, stumbling, falling, whinnying in fear. Sacagawea kept pace with the men cheerfully, even when she was chilled by rain and sleet or had to wade slowly through snow.

Safely through the Lost Trail Pass, the Corps camped briefly with a friendly band of Flathead Indians, smoking the peace pipe and trading for more horses. These people looked and dressed much like the Shoshonis, but they spoke a strange, clucking language.

As the explorers moved northward through open prairie land along the Bitterroot River, game grew scarce. The flour had given out, and Sacagawea spent her time looking for berries to share with the hungry men. No Nez Percés had appeared, and it became clear they would have to cross the dreaded Lolo Trail without their help.

As they started up the high trail, rugged mountains surrounded them. They scrambled over fallen trees which cluttered the path, and some horses slipped and rolled down a hill, smashing the equipment in their packs. Two of them were too badly hurt to continue.

On September 16 they moved into an area of knee-deep snow where the trail seemed to disappear. Their feet ached with cold in their thin moccasins. They trudged in silence or shouted above the moaning wind, eyes swimming from the blinding whiteness. Sacagawea draped a soft piece of hide over Pompy's face to protect him from the cold. Pausing at dusk, they scooped out a small clearing in the snow to camp for the night.

Hunger had become a terrible problem. Twice during the crossing they were forced to kill a colt for food. When that was gone, they ate crayfish, drank bear's oil, and even chewed tallow candles to keep from starving.

After two days of the deep snows, the captains became worried about the spirits of the Corps of Discovery. Could they be asked to fight the snows, the hunger, and the misery much longer? The next morning the captains walked beyond the edges of their camp and found a way to move down from the high ridge into a stretch of lower hills and heavy woods. The Bitterroot crossing had been made. Here at last they might find game, the Nez Percés, and the west-flowing rivers that could carry them to the ocean.

Captain Clark and six hunters pushed on ahead of the others. Soon they met a small band of the Nez Percés. The

The expedition had to find the Nez Percés and their horses. Here is a Nez Percé chief in his mountain homeland.

men wore long white buffalo robes with a braid of twisted grass around their necks. The women were dressed in tall basket hats and ankle-length dresses of sheepskins trimmed with shells.

Clark's men used sign language to show their friendship, and they were welcomed by the Nez Percés and their chief, Twisted Hair. The explorers were given baskets of dried salmon and flour made of ground camas roots. When the main party caught up with them, they were also invited to the feast.

For several days the Corps became a part of the life of the Nez Percés villages, which were strung along the west-flowing Clearwater River in what is now northern Idaho. The sick and weary travelers found the help they needed among these generous people.

Captain Lewis watched the Nez Percés paddling up and down the river in dugout canoes. Twisted Hair told him that from this point they should be able to resume water travel. A canoe camp was set up beside the Clearwater, and all the men who were not too sick were put to work making dugouts. The Nez Percés showed them how the canoes could be hollowed out faster by setting fire to the center of each log and burning out a hollow.

The explorers buried saddles, powder, and ammunition in a cache to be kept until their return. Before they turned the horses over to the Nez Percés for safekeeping, they branded them with the words: "U.S. Capt. M. Lewis."

Twisted Hair described the route to reach the ocean. They should follow the Clearwater to the Snake and from there to the Columbia. They would be going with the current, but rapids in each of the rivers would mean rough going.

On October 9 provisions were loaded into the one small canoe and four large ones they had built. There was music and dancing at a noisy afternoon farewell party. As they got ready to shove off, they discovered that the guide, Toby, and his son had left in the night without even collecting their pay. The old Shoshoni who had moved through the high country with the ease of a mountain goat was terrified at the thought of water travel. Again the Nez Percés came to their rescue. Chief Twisted Hair and another chief named Tetoharsky agreed to go with them as guides, at least as far as the Columbia.

The Clearwater flowed calmly at first, but soon the canoes were bounding through stretches of rapids. They entered the main fork of the Snake, a broad, rampaging river that cuts its way through a series of canyons. Along this river they saw fishing traps of branches used to catch salmon. They noticed Indians dipping the salmon out with nets, slitting them open, and spreading them on wooden platforms to dry.

On October 18 they reached the Columbia, known to the Indian tribes as the Great River of the West. At this eastern end it flowed at a slow, steady pace through a low sagebrush plain, while off in the distance they could see a range of high mountains. Just beyond its junction with the Walla Walla, however, the Columbia bent sharply and became a mighty, roaring river, pushing through canyons and gorges and hurtling toward the Pacific. Occasionally there were glimpses of Mount Hood, with its dazzling cap of snow.

As savage and unpredictable as a wild horse, the Columbia challenged them at every turn. It took planning and skill to come to terms with the swirling rapids, the great piles of rocks, and the waterfalls. In dangerous stretches the poor swimmers were put out of the canoes to walk on land, carrying with them valuable papers, guns, and ammunition. Friendly Indians offered their horses to haul the heavy goods around the mighty Celilo Falls, while the explorers let their canoes down over the falls with ropes and slid them over poles laid from rock to rock. In a stretch known as the Narrows, the waters were squeezed between walls of rock and shot through the channel in a whirling, powerful surge.

Day after day Sacagawea watched the spectacular beauty along the Columbia—colored cliffs washed by lacy waterfalls, giant pine and fir trees, bright mountain peaks. This was a land where a Shoshoni could feel at home.

But Sacagawea could see that the Columbia River Indians lived a different life than either her own Shoshoni people or the Hidatsas with whom she had lived. Leather tepees had given way to mat lodges, woven of rushes. Here the people were dressed with only strips of leather around their necks, their waists, and between their legs. Their eyes were

Dugouts brought the expedition safely down the powerful Columbia River.

reddened and often blinded from the bright sun reflected off the water and the mountain peaks.

Beyond the portage at Celilo Falls, Chiefs Twisted Hair and Tetoharsky asked to return to their people. They explained that they knew nothing of the Coastal languages and would no longer be able to help. Signs were increasing that the ocean was near. Sleek sea otters splashed and played along the river banks, and on the beaches they began to see the cedar canoes of the Coastal Indians. They were graceful craft, broad in the middle and tapering at both ends, with figures of men and animals carved on them. Some Indians wore sailors' coats, acquired from the traders of oceangoing ships.

Sacagawea shared the excitement of the men on November 7, 1805, when they heard the pounding of waves on rocks and guessed that they had reached the ocean at last. Their celebration had come a little early. It was not until the next day that a small exploring party reported that they had found the actual seashore.

Working in thick fog, they set up a makeshift camp, but the cliffs crowding close to the river left no suitable place. Raging waves and rain soaked their gear and water-loosened stones from the hillside tumbled down on the camp. At high tide drifting trees were washed in by the waves and threatened to smash their canoes. The river water was salty and undrinkable, and clothing and tents began to rot from being constantly wet. For eleven straight days the rains fell.

Always close by were Indians of the Coastal tribes—Chinooks and Clatsops, who rode the powerful waves in their light dugouts with skill and courage. These people were like none of the tribes Sacagawea had known. They were short, light-skinned, with pierced noses, tattooed arms, and free-flowing hair. Binding their ankles with beads had made their feet unnaturally small, while their knees were large and swollen. Their heads had been formed into a strange shape in infancy by being pressed between boards.

Captain Lewis had explored the nearby shores to find a good site for a winter fort. Clark disliked the seacoast and wanted to move far back up the Columbia, but it was necessary to stay near the river's mouth to watch for the possible arrival of a ship. President Jefferson had promised he would send one to bring them supplies for their return journey overland.

Lewis finally found a site south of the Columbia near the Oregon coast. It stood beside a stream in a thick growth of spruce safely above the level of the tide. Everyone in the party, including Sacagawea, was given a vote on the proposed site, and they quickly approved. By December 24 a crude fort had been built, which they named Fort Clatsop for a neighboring tribe.

There was safety and shelter within the cabins, but the winter at Fort Clatsop was marked by misery and boredom. Fleas swarmed over the robes on which they slept, and rain dripped on the roofs day and night. It took so long to drag game from the woods over soggy ground that it was often spoiled before it could be cooked.

Sacagawea was awakened Christmas morning by a salute of firearms and the sound of the men singing carols outside the captains' window. After breakfast there were gifts for everyone—tobacco and moccasins, stockings, and Indian baskets. Sacagawea remembered something of Christmas from the winter at Fort Mandan, so she saved two dozen

Reconstruction of Fort Clatsop, where the Corps of Discovery spent a long, dreary winter.

white weasel tails as a gift for Captain Clark. For Christmas dinner they ate spoiled elk meat and fish and a few roots.

Sacagawea's baby provided a warm touch in that dark winter of waiting. While the men rested from exploration, it was now Pompy's turn to explore. Like a bright-eyed sparrow freed from his cradleboard nest, Pompy crept into every corner of the cabins, looking and touching and learning. The men watched, smiling, as he took his first wobbly steps across the rough floor and toppled into the arms of his mother.

In order to have salt for seasoning and preserving their food, an evaporation plant was set up on the beach. One day the salt workers reported that a huge whale had died and the Indians were visiting the carcass to cut slabs of its fine blubber. Captain Clark asked Charbonneau and eleven other men to go with him the following day to the beach.

As Sacagawea listened to them make their plans, her face darkened with anger. She got to her feet and went to a far corner of the cabin. Startled, Captain Clark went to her side. What could be troubling her?

Sacagawea had been taught that it was a sign of weakness to show pain or anger. At first she was silent, disappointment gathering within her. Then softly she explained. She had traveled a long way to see the Great Waters, and, now that a monstrous fish was to be seen, she thought it "very hard" that she could not see the fish and the ocean.

Captain Clark smiled. Never once had Sacagawea been to the shore, so he arranged for her to go with the men in the canoes. The next day they paddled down to the beach by the salt works, and after traveling two more days along the shore they reached the whale. It had been stripped down to the skeleton, but they were able to purchase three hundred pounds of blubber and several gallons of whale oil from the Clatsops. Sacagawea stood long on the shore, looking beyond the curling waves that washed the beach to the unending stretch of water.

All through the expedition Captain Clark had shown gentle understanding to Sacagawea and her child. When everyone at the Fort was most bored with the skimpy winter diet, she poked into a corner of her parfleche and took out a bit of bread made from real flour. She had been saving it for Pompy, but now she offered it to the captain. The bread was a little damp, but Captain Clark ate it gratefully.

The captains always asked the same question of everyone who returned to the fort from salt making or beaver trapping. Was there any sign of the ship promised by the president? As spring approached, the question was almost never asked. No ship of any description had landed at the mouth of the Columbia, and the hope for an easy return home with new supplies had been dashed.

Another hope that had died was the president's dream of a Northwest Passage—a quick and painless pathway through the mountains to the Pacific. The expedition had proved that the mountain chain was deep and that passage through it would mean a long struggle. But the captains had learned a great deal about the best way to cross the Louisiana Purchase lands. On the return trip all the explorers would cross the Bitterroot Range together, and then the Corps would be divided into two parties. Lewis would take the most direct route to the Great Falls, while Clark's party would head to Shoshoni Cove, Three Forks, and the Yellowstone River. By dividing in this way they could explore more territory, and their report to President Jefferson would be more useful to future travelers through the Louisiana Purchase lands.

This time they would not look for Sacagawea's people. They did not have to buy horses, and Shoshoni advice on travel routes was no longer needed. With the threat of winter blizzards, crossing the Bitterroots before June 1 would be too risky, so there would be no point in leaving Fort Clatsop before April 1.

This time the explorers all knew the dangers that lay in wait for them, but they were restless to move again.

CHAPTER VIII

The Return
Journey

Late March skies were still puffy with clouds, and rain dripped from the branches. The spring sorrel was putting out its first leaves, while at Fort Clatsop the packing went on.

Shortly after noon on March 23, 1806, the rain stopped and the clearing swam with sunlight. Quickly they decided to move up the Columbia. Fort Clatsop was turned over to the Clatsop chief, and the dugouts began to push up the river.

On their way to the ocean in the fall, the west-flowing Columbia had hurled them along at a breathless speed over its rapids and between the piles of rock. Now, struggling against the current, they could feel the full fury of the river trying to drive them back. Winter rains had swollen the waters into a roaring flood. Paddles bit deep into the rushing water, and arms ached from battling the current.

Scouts warned that water travel would be impossible once they reached the Narrows and Celilo Falls. They would have to bypass this area by following a high ridge above the canyon. Pack horses would be needed—and soon—but trading had been difficult since leaving Fort Clatsop.

The calico shirts and beads and presidential medals

carried from Fort Mandan had been bartered away long before, and no ship had come with new trading goods for the return trip. Captain Clark found that the only thing he had to sell was his doctoring skill. By treating the skin sores of a village chief and curing his wife's aching back, he did manage to buy a few horses.

After leaving the coastal area, the Corps of Discovery was visited by Chief Yel-lept of the Walla Walla tribe. He promised to trade for both food and horses if they would stay for a few days at his village. Chief Yel-lept asked his people to bring fuel and food to the strangers, and soon the explorers were almost smothered with gifts. The Walla Wallas brought stems of shrubs for fuel as well as roasted fish and baskets overflowing with roots. A fine white horse was presented to Captain Clark in exchange for a few articles of clothing.

In a grand farewell, the Walla Wallas formed a big half-circle around the explorers' camp and watched them dance to the music of Cruzatte's fiddle. Then all the Walla Wallas —men, women, and children—began to sing and dance. Pompy's eyes brightened as he watched the dancing. Soon his little body began to sway and bounce to the music. Laughing, Captain Clark picked up the child, whirled around with him in his arms, and gave him a new name, "My Little Dancing Boy."

The hardest part of Corps' return journey lay ahead. When they reached Nez Percé country, they found that the hunting was so poor that the Nez Percés had been living for weeks on boiled pine moss. Even though they were suffering from hunger, the Nez Percés welcomed the explorers to their village. The captains decided to stay there until early in June because deep snow still covered the peaks of the Bitterroots. The Corps hunters shared the few animals they were able to kill with their hosts. Little Pompy suffered for many days with an abcess in his neck, but Captain Clark and Sacagawea nursed him back to health.

After crossing the Camas Flats, the Corps set out on a five-day forced march over the Lolo Trail, the same exhausting route used for the westward crossing. On the third day snows were piled high over the trail, with not even a shrub poking through as feed for the horses. Captains Lewis and Clark faced the possibility that they might become lost in these mountains. If their horses starved, they all might die, together with the records of their discoveries. Stung by their failure, they turned back, and asked the Nez Percés for help.

Returning with five dependable Nez Percé guides, they climbed the ridge once more. A firm crust of deep snow gave solid footing for the horses. The Nez Percés were confident, capable guides, able to find the trail wherever the snow had been blown away. They knew exactly where there was grass for the horses and would not let the party rest at night until they reached these grassy patches.

By June 28 they had pushed for twenty-eight miles without stripping the saddles from the horses. They made camp at noon in order to rest both the men and the animals. The meat had all been eaten, but they melted snow to boil camas roots.

Arising early the following morning, the Corps of Discovery passed safely through the last of the snows and began to ride wearily down Lolo Creek. They moved along the creek into the Bitterroot Valley to a prairie camp they named

Travellers' Rest. The dreaded crossing of the Bitterroot Mountains was over.

According to plan the Corps divided at Travellers' Rest. Captain Lewis would explore the Maria's River valley with three men after leaving six of his party at the Great Falls to help with the portage. Sacagawea, Pompy, and Charbonneau were assigned to Clark's party. They would head southeast to Shoshoni Cove, dig up the cache, and then go overland to the Yellowstone River. There they would make canoes and travel to the Missouri to meet Lewis' party. Knowing the dangers along both routes, they parted with some fear and uncertainty.

Sacagawea must have been filled with thoughts of her people as she moved with Clark's party toward her home country, even though there was no plan to make contact with the Shoshonis. They rode steadily along the Bitterroot River, and then followed an old buffalo hunters' trail over the Continental Divide and across a broad plain where she had dug roots in her childhood.

At Shoshoni Cove there was no joyous reunion for Sacagawea this time. Ten explorers headed downriver in canoes, while Sacagawea traveled with the rest of Captain Clark's party toward the Yellowstone River.

They rode through sheets of chilling rain that drenched their buckskins and slogged through oozing swampland. One July night it was so cold that ice skimmed standing water. Clouds of mosquitoes followed them all the way, and Pompy's head was peppered with puffy welts. Horses disappeared mysteriously in the night. They sent the few remaining animals ahead with three men to Fort Mandan and built canoes to take them downriver.

On this stretch of the Yellowstone, a column of rock covered with Indian carvings pokes out of the river bottom and towers above its banks. Captain Clark named it Pompy's Pillar in honor of Sacagawea's little boy and carved his own name and date at its base.

They reached the mouth of the Yellowstone August 3, and nine days later the Lewis party rejoined them. Captain Lewis was lying wounded in the bottom of one of the canoes. Cruzatte had mistaken the captain for an elk and had fired a bullet that found its mark in Lewis' buttocks.

River travel from the Yellowstone eastward went quickly. The year before paddles had dug deep in a slow struggle against the Missouri's stubborn currents. Now, headed downstream, the paddles often lay idle in the dugouts as the river carried them all the way to the Mandan and Hidatsa villages in just two days. Sun-browned and scarred, dressed in tattered buckskin, the Corps of Discovery reached the Hidatsa village on August 14, 1806. For Sacagawea this marked the end of the long journey.

How long it had been since her eyes had looked on the fields of maize, the bullboats crisscrossing the river, the earthen lodges of the village! The Hidatsa women who crowded around her were amazed that she had survived. A soft-eyed, laughing girl with a new baby had left their village a year and a half before. Now this lean, strong woman in stained and ragged buckskin moved among them with confidence. They spoke to her with warmth and a new respect.

Lewis and Clark invited the Hidatsa and Mandan chiefs to go with them to Saint Louis to meet President Jefferson, but the Indian leaders refused to travel through hostile

Pompey's Pillar National Historic Landmark.

Sioux country farther down the river. This meant that Charbonneau was no longer needed as interpreter, and so he was dismissed. The captains paid him $500.33 for his services, including the price of a horse and a lodge. Sacagawea received no pay, but Clark wanted to repay her in some way for the many contributions she had made to the success of the expedition.

Three days after their return to Fort Mandan, Captain Clark stood by his canoe saying good-bye to Toussaint Charbonneau and his family. Clark picked up Pompy and held him close. He asked the parents' permission to take the boy with him so that he might send him to school. Sacagawea smiled uncertainly and shook her head. Since Pompy was not yet weaned, he must stay with his mother one more year. She did agree that they all would go to Saint Louis the following year to accept the captain's offer.

Sacagawea stood on the banks of the Missouri with Pompy, waving as the canoes glided down the river and disappeared from sight. She had no idea what the two-year journey might mean to President Jefferson. She could not know that the expedition had opened the West for countless other explorers and settlers. At a cost of just $38,722.25, an overland route had been found to the Pacific.

The journey did mean many things for Sacagawea. It had carried her back to the land of her people, and she was stronger now than she had been at its beginning. She would never forget the captains and the brave warriors of the Corps of Discovery.

When she could see only the brown river twisting its way around the grassy hills, Sacagawea turned and walked slowly back to the village.

Epilogue

Many evenings during her journey Sacagawea had stayed near the campfire while the captains and the other explorers sat writing in their journals. Her own light, firm footsteps along the trails of America's history would later be traced through what was written in those journals. Among the scribblings would be mention of those with whom she had walked for a time—the old ones of her tribe, her brother Cameahwait, her Hidasta captors, and the stocky, blundering trader who was her husband.

When the captains and the others pushed off from the Mandan villages down the broad river toward Saint Louis, they took their pens and their journals with them. From that point Sacagawea's trail becomes blurred. Markings along the paths have been covered over by the passing years, and many things about her later life we can never know.

We do know from Captain Clark's papers that he educated Pompy. We also know that Toussaint Charbonneau and his Shoshoni wife were granted some land near Saint Louis, lived there for a short time, and then sold it to Clark.

There are records that show Charbonneau served as interpreter for other westward explorations, but none prove that Sacagawea went on any of these. They did live for a time at Fort Manuel on the border between North and South Dakota. There is some evidence that she died there. A clerk at the fort wrote on December 20, 1812: "This evening the wife of Charbonneau, a Snake squaw, died of a putrid fever. She was good and the best woman in the fort."

According to Shoshoni spoken tradition, however, Sacagawea rejoined her tribe. Many years later travelers spoke to an old Shoshoni woman with a remarkable memory of the details of the Lewis and Clark expedition. This woman was said to have died in 1884.

Did Sacagawea die at Fort Manuel at the age of 25, or did she die in her old age on the Shoshoni reservation? We may never know for sure. One thing is certain. In the memory of her people, the Shoshonis, and in the history of the United States of America a brave, strong woman named Sacagawea will live forever.

No one made a picture of Sacagawea during her lifetime, so we do not know how she looked. This is how E. S. Paxson imagined her with Lewis and Clark. Courtesy Montana Historical Society, Helena, Montana.

THE AUTHOR

Betty Westrom Skold is a former feature writer for a newspaper and has written many articles for magazines. *Sacagawea, The Story of an American Indian,* is her first published book. A graduate of Gustavus Adolphus College, she now lives in Hopkins, Minnesota with her husband and four children.

NOTE ON THE TEXT:

In most books about Sacagawea her name has been spelled "Sacajawea." However, recent research has found that Sacagawea is a more accurate phonetic spelling of her name. Pompy, which is a variation of the Indian word "Pomp" has often been spelled "Pompey." Both Sacagawea and Pompy were spelled in different ways in the journals kept by Lewis and Clark.

The photographs are reproduced through the courtesy of the Idaho Department of Commerce and Development, Idaho Historical Society, Minneapolis Public Library Athenaeum, Montana Department of Highways, National Park Service, North Dakota Park Service, Oregon State Highway Division, Smithsonian Institution National Anthropological Archives, David McKay Company, Inc. (Sacajawea: The Girl Nobody Knows, by Neta L. Frazier, 1967), and the Arthur H. Clark Company (Sacajawea, by Grace Raymond Hebard).